The Skateboarder's Guide to
Skate Parks, Half-Pipes, Bowls, and Obstacles™

TECHNICAL TERRAIN

A Skateboarder's Guide to Riding Skate Park Street Courses

Justin Hocking

The Rosen Publishing Group, Inc., New York

To Matt and Sean

Published in 2005 by The Rosen Publishing Group, Inc.
29 East 21st Street, New York, NY 10010

First Edition

Library of Congress Cataloging-in-Publication Data

Hocking, Justin.
Technical terrain: a skateboarder's guide to riding skate park street courses/Justin Hocking.—1st ed.
   p. cm.—(The skateboarder's guide to skate parks, half-pipes, bowls, and obstacles)
Includes bibliographical references and index.
ISBN 1-4042-0342-7 (lib. bdg.)
1. Skateboarding—Juvenile literature.
I. Title. II. Series: Hocking, Justin. Skateboarder's guide to skate parks, half-pipes, bowls, and obstacles.
GV859.8.H634 2005
796.22–dc22

                        2004016251

Manufactured in the United States of America

On the cover: A skateboarder does a backslide boardslide on a flat bar.

CONTENTS

INTRODUCTION

If you are like almost 10 million young people in the world, then you love to skateboard. And it's never been a better time to be a skateboarder. As the sport gains popularity and public support, hundreds of new skate parks are being built all over the country. In fact, the chances are pretty good that there's a skate park in your town or somewhere close by. The chances are also pretty good that your local skate park includes a street course. A street course is a part of a skate park that incorporates the same types of elements you might encounter on an actual street, such as ledges, curbs, and handrails.

A local skate park can offer you the chance to practice on street courses and obstacles such as this quarter-pipe.

You may already have some basic street-skating skills down and are ready to hit a street course. Or maybe you've already started to master the street course at your local park. Either way, you'll find lots of useful information in this book. We'll start off with some of the very basics and then move on to some more advanced and technical tricks. And along the way, we'll give you some fun advice about doing what skateboarding is really about—being creative and having good times with your friends.

Skateboarding has always been done in the street, even as far back as the 1940s and 1950s. The first skaters rode boards with metal wheels on streets and sidewalks. But "street skating" as we know it wasn't really invented until the early 1980s.

Skaters like Mark Gonzales, Natas Kaupus, and Tommy Guerrero were some of the true street pioneers. They were masters of the ollie and started using this trick to skate obstacles such as benches, handrails, and ledges in ways that no one previously thought was possible.

Modern street style was also influenced by freestyle skaters of the 1980s, such as Rodney Mullen, the inventor of the kick flip, the 360 flip, and many other technical variations. This book will show you how to do some of these tricks, which have become popular over the years.

CHAPTER 1

The Lowdown on Street Courses

Y ou probably already know how much fun spontaneous street skating can be. There's nothing like the freedom of rolling on your skateboard through the streets, discovering new skate spots and obstacles as you go.

Street skaters make good use of things that weren't originally designed for skateboarding—elements such as stairs, ledges, and handrails. Street skating allows you to be creative, to see a perfect skate spot where others see only a set of stairs or a bench. Street skating is almost like creating your own personal skate park wherever you go.

But there are lots of risks involved, too. You might get hassled by people who don't want you skating on their property. And if you get hurt, there might not be anyone around to offer help. For lots of people, these risks only add to the thrill of street skating.

Complicated street courses like this one simulate real-world obstacles—stairs, handrails, ramps, and curbs—without causing problems for pedestrians or local businesses. They're safer for skaters, too, who don't have to worry about cars, bicyclists, or getting a ticket from the police.

With all the positive aspects of street skating, you might wonder why you should bother with street courses in a skate park at all. They're designed to resemble actual "street spots" such as stairs, ledges, and handrails, but they're not the real thing. And you sometimes have to wait in line and pay a fee to skate. Street courses sometimes get really crowded, too, so you'll have to wait your turn and watch out for other skaters, which can get frustrating.

But skating in street courses has a lot of benefits, too. As skate park construction technology improves, some truly incredible and spacious street courses are being built in places like Chandler, Arizona, and Louisville, Kentucky. Packed with perfectly shaped quarter-pipes (ramps that are half of a half-pipe); long, smooth ledges; and uniquely shaped rails, you won't find these kinds of extraordinary concrete wonderlands on any random street. This new generation of street courses allows skaters to hit a number of different obstacles in one run, linking trick after trick after trick.

Also, if you're interested in skateboarding competitively, most street contests actually take place in skate park street courses. One of the biggest and most famous street contests takes place at the Skatepark of Tampa (SPoT). Every year SPoT organizes an amateur contest, and thousands of "young guns" from all over the country come just to enter. This is a proving ground for younger skaters seeking sponsorship by a company and hoping to move up in the ranks of the skate world.

Most skaters, though, don't take contests too seriously. No one really wants to beat another skater like players would in a basketball or football game. Most people enter just to do their best and to get a chance to hang out with other skaters. That's the other reason skate parks are great—they're a centralized meeting place where you can join up with your friends or meet new people.

Finally, street courses are generally safer than street skating. There's usually someone around to help you if you get hurt. And while you have to deal with lots of other skaters, you won't have to worry about getting hassled by police or property owners.

The truth is, skating in the actual streets and skating in street courses are both a lot of fun. Just because you do one doesn't mean you can't do the other. In fact, doing both will help you become a more well-rounded skateboarder.

The Street Course Environment

Street courses come in all sizes and shapes, and no two are exactly alike. Some are indoors. Some are outdoors. Some are made of wood, and others are made entirely of cement. Some have lots of quarter-pipes and transitions (another word for the curved part of a ramp), while others have mostly ledges and other flat obstacles. But here are a few elements that you will find in just about every street course:

1. **Pyramids:** Pyramids are made up of several banks placed together to form the shape of a pyramid. Most skate park pyramids, though, have a flat top instead of the pointy tip you see on Egyptian pyramids.

2. **Banks:** Banks are flat, slanted obstacles, like ramps without the curve. Banks help you maintain speed in a street course, and they are a good place to try some more technical tricks.

3. **Ledges:** Ledges are square, boxlike obstacles that are good for grinds and slides. Most ledges are made out of concrete, but some are a combination of wood and metal. They're generally between 0.5 feet and 3 feet (0.15 and 0.9 meters) tall.

4. **Manual pads**: Sometimes known as a wheelie, a manual is a trick where you ride balancing only on your back wheels (unless you're doing a nose manual, where you balance only on your front wheels). Manual pads are small, flat boxes that you ollie onto and then manual across.

5. **Rails**: Rails are similar to ledges, but they're made out of metal. A flat bar is a type of small, flat rail, while a handrail is a bigger type of rail that usually descends down a set of stairs.

6. **Quarter-pipes:** A quarter-pipe is a type of ramp with a transition. Like banks, quarter-pipes also help you maintain your speed. They're also good for all sorts of tricks such as grinds, stalls, and airs.

This skater is doing a Smith grind down a handrail at a Skatepark of Tampa (SPoT) contest. SPoT changes its courses periodically, hosts contests, and offers lessons to aspiring skaters.

Watch and Learn (and Stay Safe)

If you read this book carefully and put in some major practice time, you'll pick up most of the tricks we cover. Unfortunately, we can only cover a handful of tricks, even though there are hundreds more to try and many different ways of doing each individual trick, depending on the type of obstacle you hit. So an equally important way to learn about skateboarding is to actually watch other people in action.

When you show up at a new street course, don't just get right in the mix and begin skating. Instead, take a seat and just watch for a while.

SOME OF THE WORLD'S BEST STREET COURSES

Louisville Extreme Park (Louisville, Kentucky): One of the largest outdoor public skate parks in the world, the Louisville park features a gigantic concrete street course area, with a large variety of banks, ledges, manual pads, and so on. Stadium-style lighting allows this unique park to remain open twenty-four hours a day.

Rye Airfield (Rye, New Hampshire): This enormous indoor skate park boasts more than 50,000 square feet (4,645 sq m) of skateable terrain. By offering three separate street courses—one each for beginner, intermediate, and advanced skaters—this park has something for skaters of all abilities. The advanced street course area also features a unique rainbow-shaped ledge.

Skatepark of Tampa (Tampa, Florida): Though the street course in the Tampa park is relatively small, it's filled with modern, skater-built pyramids, ledges, quarter-pipes, and so on. This makes it the perfect spot for the famous annual Skatepark of Tampa amateur and pro contests.

Fossil Creek Skate Park (Fort Collins, Colorado): Unlike many street courses that feature quarter-pipes and other curved surfaces that you rarely find at an actual street spot, the Fossil Creek Skate Park was designed to look like an actual urban plaza, with staircases and ledges of varying sizes. The park also features a very unique "gap" where advanced skaters can jump over a small reservoir that's filled with water!

11

Pay attention to the good skaters and how they use the street course obstacles. See where they go and what kind of lines they take. This will also help you stay safe once you actually start riding the course because it's common knowledge that the majority of skateboard-related injuries happen to people who are just starting out. Instead of just rolling blindly into the skate park, which can lead to a major collision, you'll have a better sense of where the other skaters will be going.

Another important way to keep yourself safe is to always wear pads and a helmet. Some skate parks require pads and some don't, but we recommend you wear them all the time.

Basic Street Course Tricks

You probably already have most of the basics down, like ollies, manuals, and maybe even kick flips. So now you're ready to start trying these tricks on some street course obstacles and also to learn some more advanced tricks.

The tricks in this book are divided into three categories: basic, intermediate, and advanced. It's important to start out with the basics, like learning to 50-50 on a ledge, because you'll need to have that down before you try harder moves like a 50-50 down a handrail, which is a more difficult form of the same trick. That's how skateboarding works—it's a constant progression, where learning one trick gives you the foundation for learning another. But don't worry about getting the hardest tricks down. Skateboarding is really just about having fun and moving at your own pace.

Ollie on a Pyramid

Most street courses have some sort of pyramid, and they're often the centerpiece of the course. Pyramids are a popular place for more technical flip tricks (we'll cover these later in the book), which require you to know how to ollie, so it's good to learn a basic ollie first:

OLLIE ON A PYRAMID

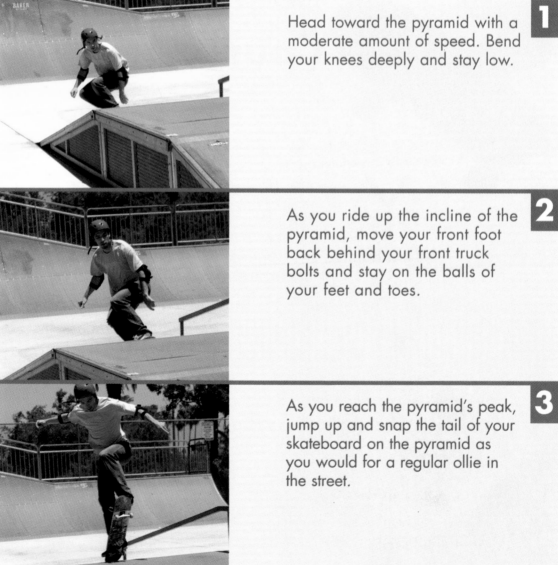

1. Head toward the pyramid with a moderate amount of speed. Bend your knees deeply and stay low.

2. As you ride up the incline of the pyramid, move your front foot back behind your front truck bolts and stay on the balls of your feet and toes.

3. As you reach the pyramid's peak, jump up and snap the tail of your skateboard on the pyramid as you would for a regular ollie in the street.

4 When you reach your maximum height in the air above the pyramid, tuck your knees up toward your body and use your feet to lift the board up as high as you can.

5 Spot your landing, straighten your legs out, and set the board back down.

Ollie to Fakie on a Bank

Doing a trick to fakie means you ride away backward. Flat banks are a good place to do more technical tricks, so it's good to learn some bank basics first like ollie to fakie. Try these on a small, shallow bank first, and then work it up to steeper, taller banks.

1 Ride up the bank with your knees bent. Pop an ollie at the top of the bank.

(continued on page 16)

2 Just before you reach the top, ollie up above, or higher than, the top of the bank.

3 As you begin to land, try to set your front and back wheels down at the same time. Put a little extra weight on your front foot as you land. Keep your shoulders straight, and as you start to roll backward down the bank, simply turn your neck and head 90 degrees, so you can see where you're going.

4 Bend your knees and stay low as you roll down and back onto the flat surface.

50-50 Grind on a Ledge

This is the first trick that most people learn on a ledge. You can try it on a small curb first and then work your way up to higher ledges. When you're first getting the hang of the 50-50, you don't need much speed. But once you get comfortable, rolling up to the ledge with more speed will help you grind faster and farther.

1 Approach the ledge with moderate speed and at a slight angle. You should be on the balls of your feet and your toes, and your front foot should be back behind your truck bolts for maximum snap in your ollie.

2 Get really low and then ollie up to the ledge. Guide your board into place, so that you set both trucks down on the edge of the ledge.

3 Bend your knees slightly, and keep your hips and shoulders parallel to the ledge as you grind.

4 As you reach the end of the ledge, put a little extra weight on your heels, press down slightly on your tail, and lift your front trucks off. Set the board down smoothly on the ground, and bend your knees to absorb the shock.

Ollie to Manual on a Manual Pad

As we mentioned before, a manual in the street is like a wheelie, where you roll while balancing on your back wheels only, with your front wheels up in the air. They're easy on the flat ground, but it takes more skill to ollie into a manual on a street obstacle.

OLLIE TO MANUAL ON A MANUAL PAD

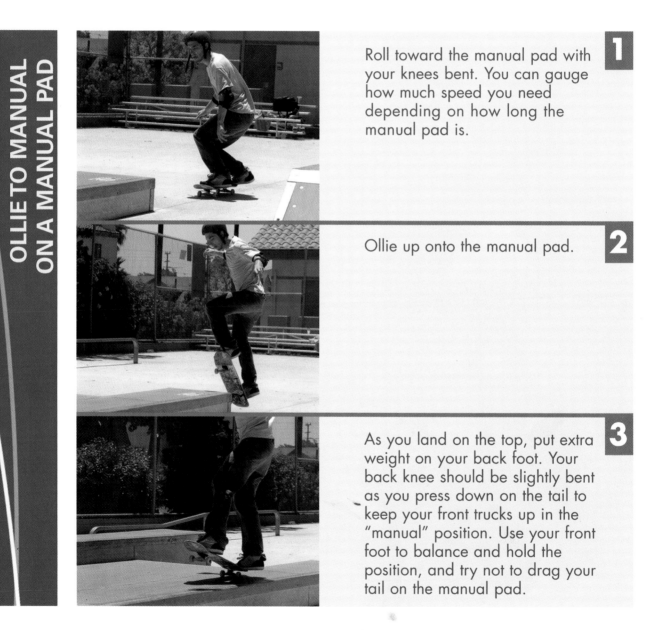

1 Roll toward the manual pad with your knees bent. You can gauge how much speed you need depending on how long the manual pad is.

2 Ollie up onto the manual pad.

3 As you land on the top, put extra weight on your back foot. Your back knee should be slightly bent as you press down on the tail to keep your front trucks up in the "manual" position. Use your front foot to balance and hold the position, and try not to drag your tail on the manual pad.

4 As you roll off the end of the manual pad, press down slightly on your tail, but don't snap your tail on the ground like you would for an ollie. Once you land back on the ground, set your front wheels down and bend your knees a little as you ride away.

Backside Boardslide on a Flat Bar

The backside boardslide is a classic trick that looks stylish when done right. When you're first learning, try sliding just the last foot or so of a short, flat bar. Once you get more confident with this trick, approach the bar with more speed to slide the entire length of the bar.

1 Roll up toward the flat bar with medium speed, with your shoulders parallel to the obstacle.

2 As you reach the middle of the bar, snap an ollie, turning the board 90 degrees toward your heels. Make sure you ollie high enough to get your front trucks and wheels over the bar.

(continued on page 20)

19

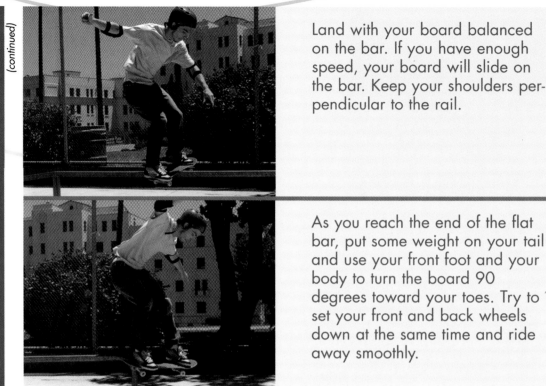

3 Land with your board balanced on the bar. If you have enough speed, your board will slide on the bar. Keep your shoulders perpendicular to the rail.

4 As you reach the end of the flat bar, put some weight on your tail and use your front foot and your body to turn the board 90 degrees toward your toes. Try to set your front and back wheels down at the same time and ride away smoothly.

Dropping in on a Quarter-Pipe

Start out on a smaller quarter-pipe, one that's about 4 or 5 feet (1.2 or 1.5 m) high. Make sure no one's in the way when you first drop in. This is a good one to learn before you move on, because dropping in on a ramp helps you get the speed you'll need for some of the more advanced tricks.

1 Set your tail down on the coping of the ramp with the trucks and wheels hanging over the edge. Place your back foot on the tail to keep the board in place. Keep your knees slightly bent.

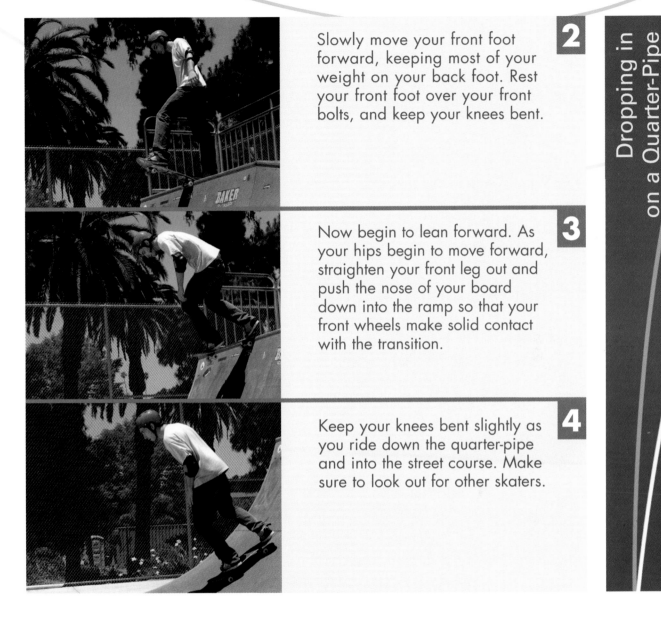

2 Slowly move your front foot forward, keeping most of your weight on your back foot. Rest your front foot over your front bolts, and keep your knees bent.

3 Now begin to lean forward. As your hips begin to move forward, straighten your front leg out and push the nose of your board down into the ramp so that your front wheels make solid contact with the transition.

4 Keep your knees bent slightly as you ride down the quarter-pipe and into the street course. Make sure to look out for other skaters.

Dropping in on a Quarter-Pipe

Congratulations on your first drop in! Dropping in on a quarter-pipe is also a good first step for learning to skate on a half-pipe, which is basically just two quarter-pipes connected with a flat bottom. For more info on skating half-pipes, check out our book *Rippin' Ramps: A Skate-boarder's Guide to Riding Half-Pipes.*

HOW TO PLAY S.K.A.T.E.

So now you have a few tricks down in the street course, right? If so, you're ready to play a few rounds of S.K.A.T.E. To play, you need at least two other friends who are at about the same skating skill level as yourself. It's also a good idea to play S.K.A.T.E. when the skate park isn't too crowded, or you might end up getting in people's way.

You play S.K.A.T.E. pretty much the same way you play H.O.R.S.E. with a basketball. First, you have to establish an order, so that the same person always goes first, second, third, and so on. Once you're ready to go, the first skater rides into the street course and does the trick of his/her choice. If the first skater makes the trick, then the second skater has to do the exact same trick. If the second skater makes it, the third skater has to do it, too. It goes on like this until someone misses the trick, which gives him or her an "S." Then it starts all over, and the next skater gets to set a trick.

As soon as anyone gets all five of the letters—S.K.A.T.E.—he or she is out. The winner of the game is the last person left.

Once you learn these basic tricks, practice until you can land them on nearly every try. Unless you perfect the basic tricks, you'll find it hard to progress to the intermediate and advanced tricks. The intermediate and advanced tricks are all based on the basic tricks. These first steps serve as a foundation for the tricks to come in this book.

CHAPTER 3

Intermediate Street Course Tricks

Now that you have some basic tricks wired, you're ready for some harder moves. Most of these tricks build directly on the beginner tricks. Getting these intermediate tricks down will help you learn the most advanced tricks, too. And remember, you don't have to do everything exactly the way we explain it. Don't be afraid to try things differently or to add your own variations to tricks.

Backside 180 Ollie on a Pyramid

To do this trick, you should be comfortable doing 180 ollies on the flat ground. This is a fun trick, and it's a good one to learn before you try more advanced tricks.

BACKSIDE 180 OLLIE ON A PYRAMID

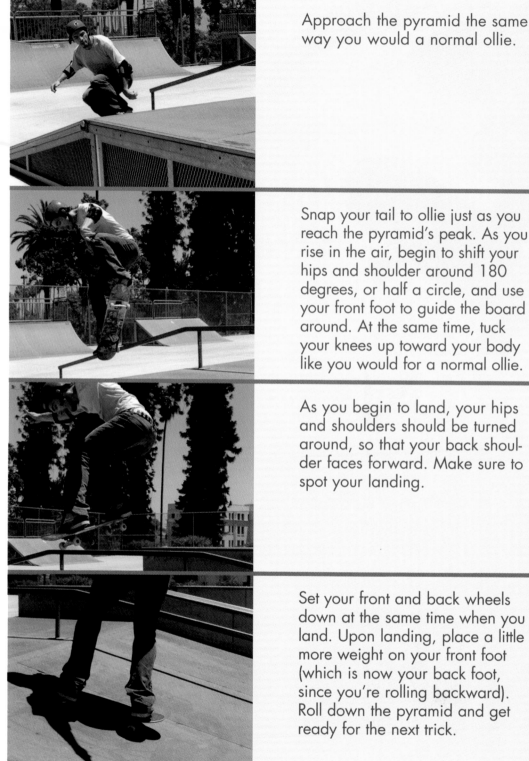

1 Approach the pyramid the same way you would a normal ollie.

2 Snap your tail to ollie just as you reach the pyramid's peak. As you rise in the air, begin to shift your hips and shoulder around 180 degrees, or half a circle, and use your front foot to guide the board around. At the same time, tuck your knees up toward your body like you would for a normal ollie.

3 As you begin to land, your hips and shoulders should be turned around, so that your back shoulder faces forward. Make sure to spot your landing.

4 Set your front and back wheels down at the same time when you land. Upon landing, place a little more weight on your front foot (which is now your back foot, since you're rolling backward). Roll down the pyramid and get ready for the next trick.

Kick Flip to Fakie on a Flat Bank

To do this trick, you should be able to do kick flips on flat ground. Also, make sure to warm up with a few simple ollie to fakies on the bank. Try this trick low on the bank at first and then work your way up higher and higher.

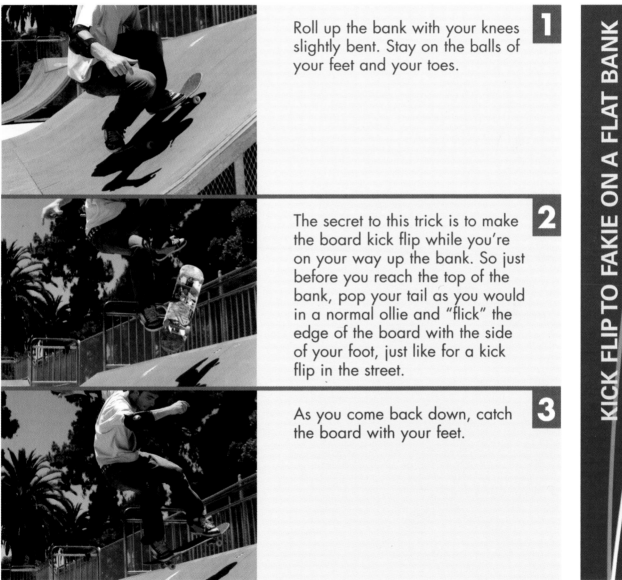

1 Roll up the bank with your knees slightly bent. Stay on the balls of your feet and your toes.

2 The secret to this trick is to make the board kick flip while you're on your way up the bank. So just before you reach the top of the bank, pop your tail as you would in a normal ollie and "flick" the edge of the board with the side of your foot, just like for a kick flip in the street.

3 As you come back down, catch the board with your feet.

(continued on page 26)

KICK FLIP TO FAKIE ON A FLAT BANK

After you catch the board, set it back down with a little extra weight on your front foot. Stay low as you roll down.

Boardslide Down a Handrail

The boardslide down a handrail is a more advanced version of the boardslide on a flat bar. This is a little hard though because the handrail is on an angle and requires a little more balance. Here's how to do it:

BOARDSLIDE DOWN A HANDRAIL

Roll up to the ledge the same way you would for a boardslide on a flat bar. Stay on the balls of your feet and your toes, and get low before you pop your ollie.

As you snap your ollie, quickly turn your hips and shoulders 90 degrees. Then lift your front truck over the rail.

Balance your board on top of the rail. Lean forward a little bit as you slide, but not too much or you'll fall forward. **3**

As you begin to reach the end of the rail, turn your board off with your front foot and by rotating your hips and shoulders 90 degrees. Set the board back down and ride away. **4**

Boardslide Down a Handrail

Nose Manual on a Manual Pad

Make sure you're comfortable doing a nose manual in the street before trying it on a manual pad. This one takes a lot of balance and finesse, so don't get frustrated if it takes a while to learn.

Approach the manual pad at medium speed. **1**

NOSE MANUAL ON A MANUAL PAD

(continued on page 28)

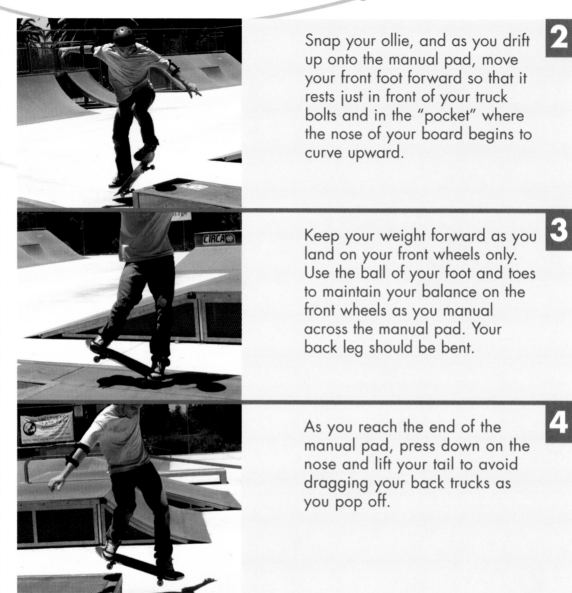

Nose Manual on a Manual Pad *(continued)*

2 Snap your ollie, and as you drift up onto the manual pad, move your front foot forward so that it rests just in front of your truck bolts and in the "pocket" where the nose of your board begins to curve upward.

3 Keep your weight forward as you land on your front wheels only. Use the ball of your foot and toes to maintain your balance on the front wheels as you manual across the manual pad. Your back leg should be bent.

4 As you reach the end of the manual pad, press down on the nose and lift your tail to avoid dragging your back trucks as you pop off.

Nollie to Lipslide

You should already be comfortable with lipslides before you try this trick. And you should be able to do a nollie, or an ollie using the nose of the board, on the street.

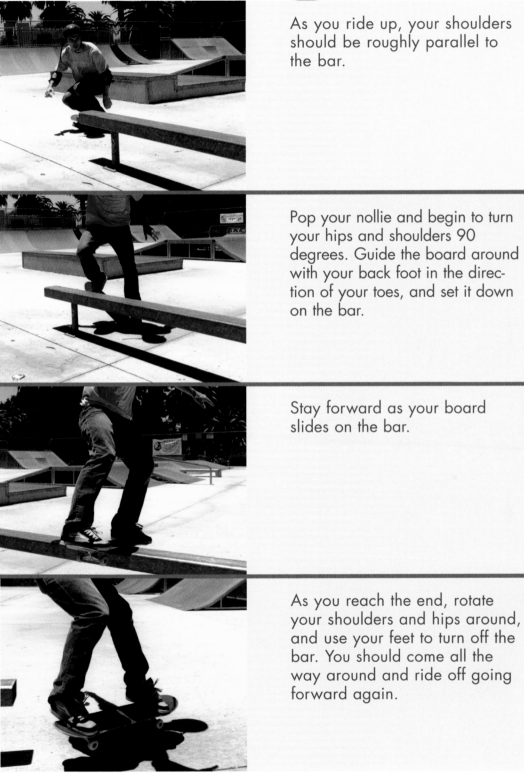

1 As you ride up, your shoulders should be roughly parallel to the bar.

2 Pop your nollie and begin to turn your hips and shoulders 90 degrees. Guide the board around with your back foot in the direction of your toes, and set it down on the bar.

3 Stay forward as your board slides on the bar.

4 As you reach the end, rotate your shoulders and hips around, and use your feet to turn off the bar. You should come all the way around and ride off going forward again.

NOLLIE TO LIPSLIDE

Axle Stall on a Quarter-Pipe

"Axle" is another name for your truck, so when you do an axle stall, you rest, or stall, your trucks on the top of the coping, rather than grinding. Axle stalls are a good "set-up" trick—they give you a chance to rest for a moment and then get plenty of speed as you drop back into the quarter-pipe.

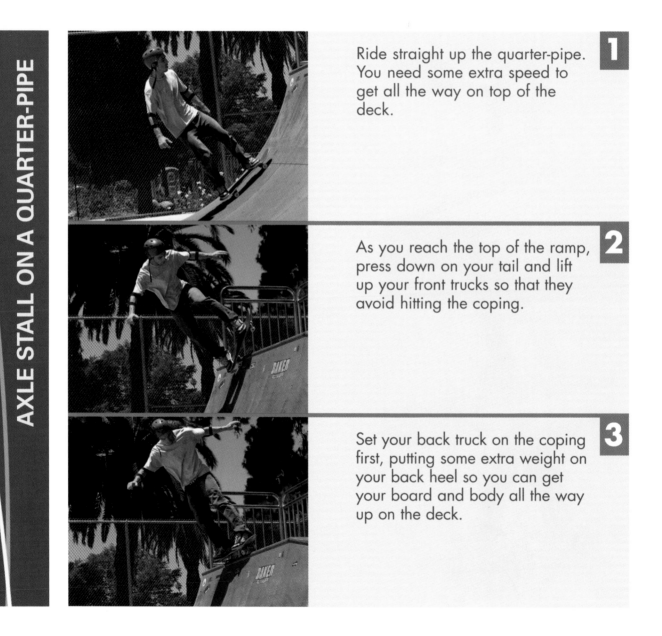

AXLE STALL ON A QUARTER-PIPE

1 Ride straight up the quarter-pipe. You need some extra speed to get all the way on top of the deck.

2 As you reach the top of the ramp, press down on your tail and lift up your front trucks so that they avoid hitting the coping.

3 Set your back truck on the coping first, putting some extra weight on your back heel so you can get your board and body all the way up on the deck.

4 Once your back truck is resting on the coping, use it as your pivot point, bringing your shoulders and hips around so they're parallel with the coping below you. Set your front truck down, keeping the weight on your heels and your body leaning in toward the ramp.

5 After you stall for a second, press down on your tail with the toes of your back foot, lean forward, turn off the coping, and ride back into the ramp.

Skateboard Trivia

Skateboarding has a long and interesting history. Try to guess the answers to some of the following trivia questions. Once you learn the answers, impress your friends with your new skate knowledge.

1) Which pro skater invented the ollie?

2) Which pro skater was the first to do an ollie down the 20-foot-high (6 m) "leap of faith"?

3) One of the most famous street spots ever was called Love Park. In what East Coast city was Love Park located?

4) Who invented the kick flip?

5) Who holds the world record for highest air on a ramp (18 feet [5.5 m])?

6) Which pro skater first landed a 900-degree spin on a vert ramp?

7) Who was the first professional female street skater?

8) Who invented the McTwist?

9) Which professional skater is nicknamed TNT?

10) What do you call the trick where the grip tape side of your board slides on the ledge, while you stand on the bottom of the board?

Answers:

1) Allen Gelfand 2) Jamie Thomas 3) Philadelphia 4) Rodney Mullen 5) Danny Way 6) Tony Hawk 7) Elissa Steamer 8) Mike McGill 9) Tony Trujillo 10) The dark slide

CHAPTER 4
Advanced Street Course Tricks

So now you have some beginner and intermediate tricks down. You have some new slides, grinds, and flips under your belt. That's good. This next round of tricks can be pretty tough. Some of them might take weeks and even months to master. Skateboarding isn't easy, but that's what makes it so rewarding.

Backside Tailslide on a Ledge

You should have 50-50s down before you try tailslides. This is another good trick to learn on a curb first. The backside tailside is a stylish trick. Once you master it, you can try variations like the kick flip to tailslide and tailside to fakie.

BACKSIDE TAILSLIDE ON A LEDGE

1 Approach the ledge at a slight angle and at medium speed, ready to snap your ollie.

2 Snap your ollie and turn about 90 degrees in the direction of your toes. Raise your tail just above the height of the ledge.

3 Lock your tail on the ledge and balance in that position as you slide across.

4 Complete your spin, set the board back down, and bend your knees slightly as you roll away.

Bluntslide on a Ledge

Bluntslides are among the most difficult of all the ledge tricks. Try this on a regular curb before you attempt it on a ledge. Bluntslides can also be done on flat bars or even handrails.

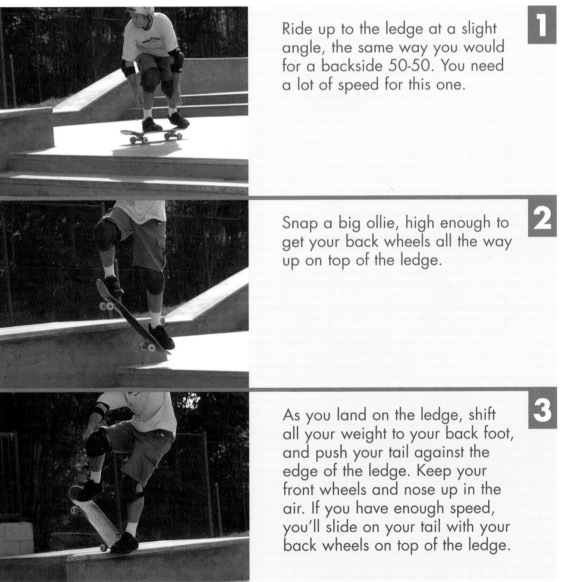

1 Ride up to the ledge at a slight angle, the same way you would for a backside 50-50. You need a lot of speed for this one.

2 Snap a big ollie, high enough to get your back wheels all the way up on top of the ledge.

3 As you land on the ledge, shift all your weight to your back foot, and push your tail against the edge of the ledge. Keep your front wheels and nose up in the air. If you have enough speed, you'll slide on your tail with your back wheels on top of the ledge.

(continued on page 36)

BLUNTSLIDE ON A LEDGE

4 As you reach the end of the ledge, do a slight ollie out of the bluntslide position and slightly press down on the front of the board. Then use your back foot to pop the board off the ledge and level it out, while turning your shoulders and hips to face forward.

Kick Flip to Manual on a Manual Pad

This is a good one to try once you have kick flips and manuals wired. And you can try adding variations as you roll off the manual pad, like a 180 ollie, a pop shove-it, or even another kick flip. Keep in mind that these kinds of technical manual tricks are really difficult and may take you countless tries to learn.

KICK FLIP TO MANUAL ON A MANUAL PAD

1 Roll up to the manual pad the same way you would for a regular ollie to manual.

2 Just like with a normal kick flip, you have to slide your foot up the front of the board as you ollie, and "flick" the edge of the board to make it flip. You'll have to ollie a little higher than usual to get up on the manual pad.

3 Try to catch the board with your back foot first. This makes it easier to put a little extra weight on your tail, which will put you in the manual position as you land on the manual pad.

4 Manual across the pad without setting your tail down. Ride off the pad, land on the pavement, and skate away.

Krooked Grind on a Flat Bar

The krooked is one of the most technical grinds. To do a krooked grind, you have to balance on your front trucks and nose while grinding. So, having an ollie to nose manual mastered on a manual pad will help give you the basic motions for this trick.

1 Approach the flat bar backside and at a slight angle.

(continued on page 38)

37

2 Pop an ollie, and slide your front foot up to the right side of your board's nose.

3 As your front trucks make contact with the bar, straighten out your front leg and press down on your nose. Keep your back knee bent. This should put you in the krooked position.

4 As you come to the end of the bar, put some extra pressure on your nose, level the board out, and turn off the bar.

50-50 Grind on a Handrail

Handrails are some of the most difficult and dangerous skate obstacles. But a lot of skate parks have smaller handrails that are good to learn on. And before you try this trick, make sure you have 50-50s mastered on ledges and flat bars.

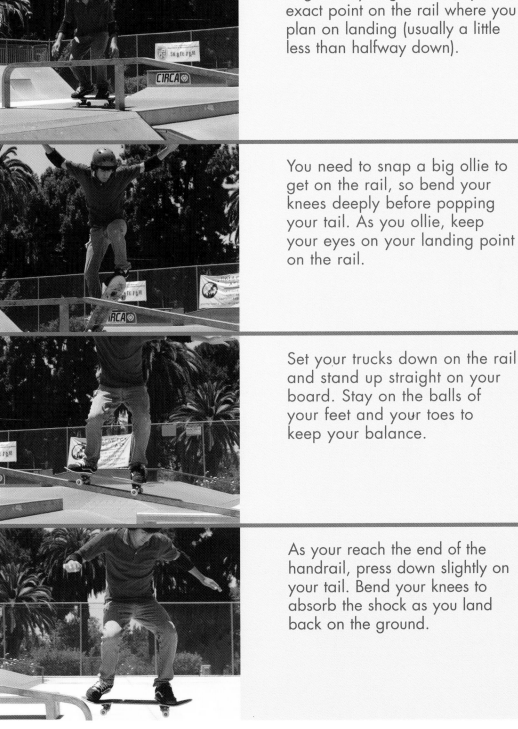

1 Roll up to the ledge at a slight angle. As you get closer, spot the exact point on the rail where you plan on landing (usually a little less than halfway down).

2 You need to snap a big ollie to get on the rail, so bend your knees deeply before popping your tail. As you ollie, keep your eyes on your landing point on the rail.

3 Set your trucks down on the rail and stand up straight on your board. Stay on the balls of your feet and your toes to keep your balance.

4 As your reach the end of the handrail, press down slightly on your tail. Bend your knees to absorb the shock as you land back on the ground.

50-50 GRIND ON A HANDRAIL

Pivot to Fakie on a Quarter-Pipe

The pivot to fakie is a stylish and difficult trick. It's a good set-up trick for more street-oriented tricks where you need to be going backward. You should have axle stalls wired before you try this trick (a pivot is basically just an axle stall where you balance on your back truck only).

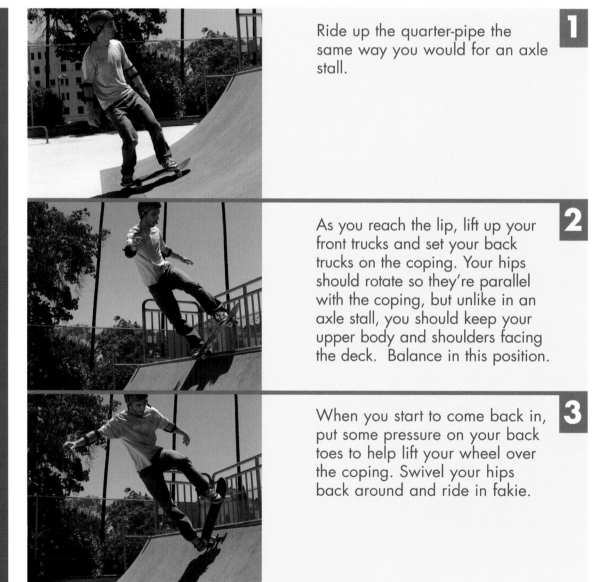

PIVOT TO FAKIE ON A QUARTER-PIPE

1 Ride up the quarter-pipe the same way you would for an axle stall.

2 As you reach the lip, lift up your front trucks and set your back trucks on the coping. Your hips should rotate so they're parallel with the coping, but unlike in an axle stall, you should keep your upper body and shoulders facing the deck. Balance in this position.

3 When you start to come back in, put some pressure on your back toes to help lift your wheel over the coping. Swivel your hips back around and ride in fakie.

4 Keep your shoulders straight and look over your back shoulder as you ride in and set up for your next trick.

Instead of just doing one single trick, street courses allow you to do a variety of tricks on all sorts of obstacles. It's fun to see how many you can put together in a single line. Depending on how your street course is set up, you might try a manual on a manual pad, and then grind down a ledge or ollie a gap. It's all up to you, of course. The great thing about skateboarding is that there are no rules and no fixed routines. The most important thing is to be creative and have fun.

GLOSSARY

backside A style associated with any number of tricks in which you turn toward your toes.

bluntslide A trick in which you slide with the board resting on a ledge in the position where the wheels are on top of the ledge.

coping Metal piping that is attached to the edge of a ramp to allow for grinds and slides.

fakie Riding a skateboard in a backward position.

50-50 A trick in which both trucks are resting firmly on a ledge.

flip trick A trick in which the board flips.

grind Any trick in which the trucks of the skateboard slide across a surface.

kick flip A trick in which the board flips widthwise one full rotation.

line The series of tricks a skater does.

lipslide A slide in which the skater ollies over the rail and lands in the opposite position of a normal slide.

ollie A trick in which the skater jumps with the board by snapping the tail on the ground.

180 ollie A trick in which the skater ollies and turn the board 180 degrees to land with the skateboard moving in the opposite position.

pop shove-it A trick in which the skater ollies and turns the board 180 degrees while the skater remains in the same position.

slide A trick in which the bottom of the skateboard slides across a surface such as a ledge or rail.

tail The upward-curving back end of a skateboard.

360 flip A kick flip in which the board also turns 360 degrees.

truck The part of a skateboard that attaches the wheels to the board.

Mission Valley YMCA
5505 Friar's Road
San Diego, CA 92110
(619) 298-3576
Web site: http://missionvalley.ymca.org

Rye Airfield
170 Lafayette Road
Rye, NH 03870
(603) 964-2800
e-mail: info@ryeairfield.com
Web site: http://www.ryeairfield.com

Skatelab Indoor Skatepark and Museum
4226 Valley Fair Street
Simi Valley, CA 93063
(805) 578-0040
e-mail: info@skatelab.com
Web site: http://www.skatelab.com

Skatepark of Tampa
4215 East Columbus Drive
Tampa, FL 33605
(813) 621-6793
e-mail: info@skateparkoftampa.com
Web site: http://www.skateparkoftampa.com

Vans Skateboard Camp
50 S.E. Scott Street
Bend, OR 97702
(800) 334-4272
Web site: http://www.vansskatecamp.com

Woodward Camp
P.O. Box 93
134 Sports Camp Drive, Route 45
Woodward, PA 16882
(814) 349-5633
Web site: http://www.woodwardcamp.com

Web Sites

Due to the changing nature of Internet links, the Rosen Publishing Group, Inc., has developed an online list of Web sites related to the subject of this book. This site is updated regularly. Please use this link to access the list:

http://www.rosenlinks.com/skgu/tete

FOR FURTHER READING

Brooke, Michael. *The Concrete Wave: The History of Skateboarding*. Toronto, ON: Warwick Publishing, 1999.

Doeden, Matt. *Skateparks: Grab Your Skateboard*. Mankato, MN: Capstone Press, 2002.

Thrasher Magazine. *Thrasher: Insane Terrain*. New York: Universe Publishing, 2001.

Weyland, Jocko. *The Answer Is Never*. New York: Grove Press, 2002.

BIBLIOGRAPHY

Brooke, Michael. *The Concrete Wave.* Toronto, ON: Warwick
  Publishing, 1999.
Skateboard.com. "Camps." Retrieved January 24, 2004 (http://www
  .skateboard.com/frontside/GetLocal/camps/default.asp).
Vansskatecamp.com. "Skate—Summer 2004." Retrieved January 24,
  2004 (http://www.vansskatecamp.com/index.htm).

INDEX

About the Author

Justin Hocking lives and skateboards in New York City. He is also an editor of the book *Life and Limb: Skateboarders Write from the Deep End*, published in 2004 by Soft Skull Press.

Credits

Cover, pp. 14-21, 24-31, 34-41 ©Tony Donaldson/Icon SMI/The Rosen Publishing Group; p. 4 © Syracuse Nespapers/The Image Works; p. 7 Courtesy of Site Design Group, Inc./www.sitedesigngroup.com and Site Skate Parks, Inc./www.siteskateparks.com; p.10 courtesy of Skatepark of Tampa/www.skateparkoftampa.com.

Designer: Les Kanturek; Editor: Nicholas Croce;
Photo Researcher: Rebecca Anguin-Cohn